Animal Habitats

Ocean Habitats

Written by Noah Leatherland

KidHaven Publishing

Published in 2025 by
KidHaven Publishing, an Imprint of
Greenhaven Publishing, LLC
2544 Clinton St., Buffalo, NY 14224

Written by: Noah Leatherland
Edited by: Elise Carraway
Designed by: Ker Ker Lee

Cataloging-in-Publication Data

Names: Leatherland, Noah, 1999-.
Title: Ocean habitats / Noah Leatherland.
Description: Buffalo, NY : KidHaven Publishing, 2025. | Series: Animal habitats | Includes glossary and index.
Identifiers: ISBN 9781534548244 (pbk.) | ISBN 9781534548251 (library bound) | ISBN 9781534548268 (ebook)
Subjects: LCSH: Marine animals--Juvenile literature. | Marine ecology--Juvenile literature.
Classification: LCC QL122.2 L43 2025 | DDC 591.77--dc23

Manufactured in the United States of America

CPSIA compliance information: Batch #CSKH25
For further information contact Greenhaven Publishing LLC at 1-844-317-7404.

Photo Credits. Images are courtesy of Shutterstock.com. With thanks to Getty Images, Thinkstock Photo and iStockphoto.
Recurring – WinWin artlab, Sensvector.
Cover – Vladyslav Karpovych, Eric Isselee, losw, Alfmaler, sunwart. 2–3 – Neil Bromhall. 4–5 – Anne Coatesy, Damsea. 6–7 – COULANGES, Nina Milton. 8–9 – haveseen, takayuki. 10–11 – Ethan Daniels, NatureDiver, raulbaldean. 12–13 – Gerald Robert Fischer, RLS Photo. 14–15 – Goinyk Production, videotrinkets. 16–17 – elena_photo_soul, Stefano Bolognini. 18–19 – DiveSpin.Com, Jack FotoVerse. 20–21 – Grace Chan, jushpx. 22–23 – Eivor Kuchta, IrinaK.

Contents

Words that look like <u>this</u> can be found in the glossary on page 24.

What Is a Habitat?

Habitats are where living things make their homes. A habitat has everything that animals and plants need to survive. This includes food, water, and shelter.

a rat in a forest habitat

Oceans

The oceans are still being explored, and new animals are still being discovered.

Most of the planet is covered in water. There are lots of different animals that can be found in the oceans. They all have different ways of surviving in their watery habitats.

Seahorse

Under the water, predators can come from any direction. Seahorses have eyes that can move in different directions from each other. This means they can watch out for predators while searching for food.

Seahorses have long snouts to suck up their prey. They can move their heads around very quickly to catch food floating past. This is very helpful for eating tiny sea creatures such as zooplankton.

Seahorses are usually found in calm waters near seagrass.

Manta Ray

Manta rays are filter feeders. This means they take water in through their mouths, eat the tiny creatures in it, then push the rest of the water out. Their lobes push prey into their mouths.

Sometimes, manta rays hunt together. Manta rays group up to swim in a circle to create a whirlpool. Their prey gets trapped in the whirlpool, which makes it easier for the manta rays to eat them.

Manta rays can be found in oceans all over the world.

Starfish

Starfish stick to rocks with their special tube feet. They do not move very quickly. So, to protect themselves, starfish have very hard, bony skin that is difficult for predators to get through.

tube feet

Starfish can be found around rocky areas in the ocean.

If a starfish is harmed by a predator, it can regenerate. This means that if a starfish loses parts of its body, it can grow them back.

Lobster

Lobsters have hairs on their legs and feet that can smell things. This is helpful when finding food to eat. Lobsters can even find tiny pieces of food that have dissolved in the water.

Lobsters live along the ocean floor.

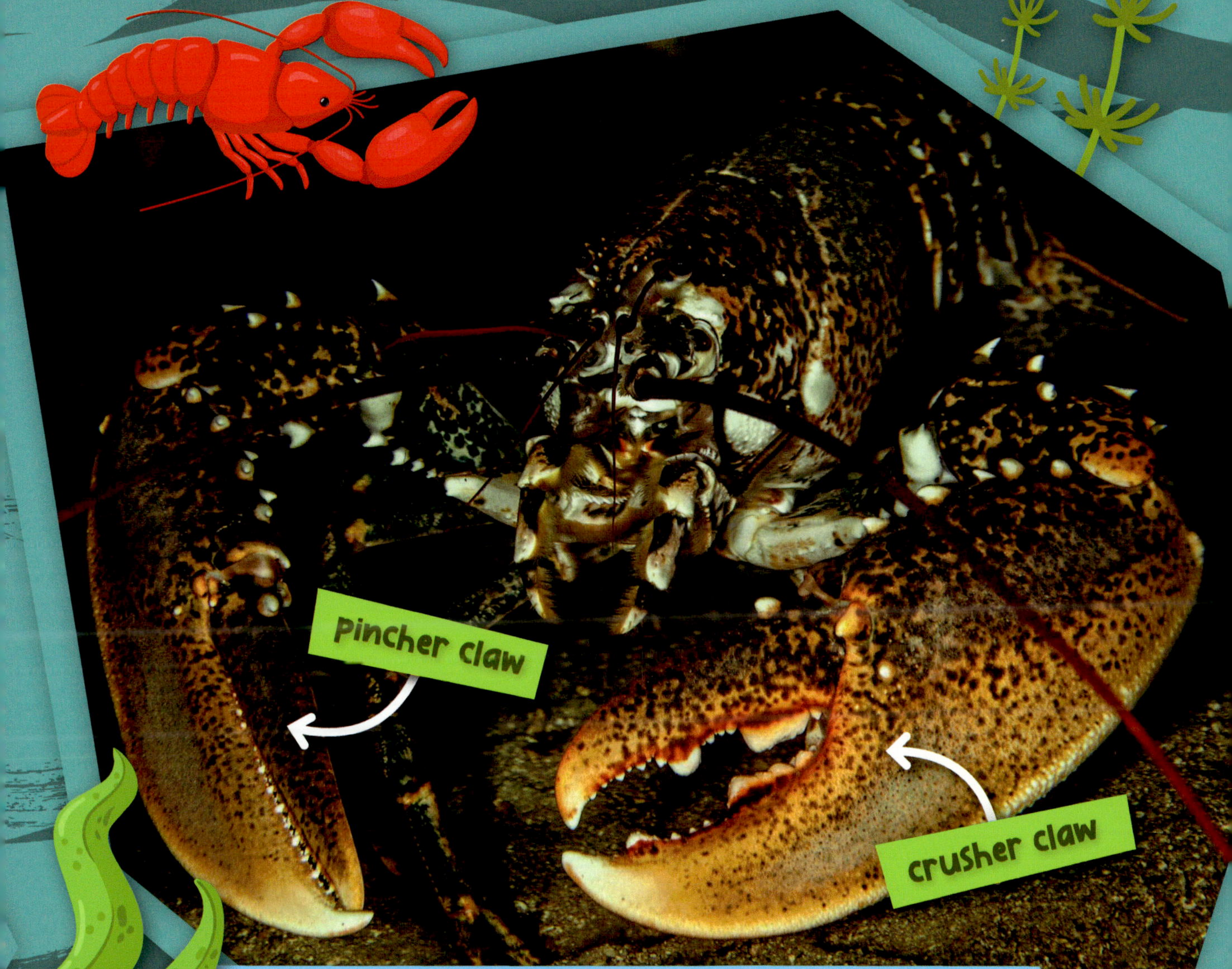

One of the lobster's claws is for crushing, which helps them break the shells of other creatures. The other claw is for pinching, so the lobster can pick out food and eat it.

Coral Polyps

Coral reefs are usually found in warm water near land.

Corals may look just like colorful rocks, but they are actually living creatures. The hard shells of many coral polyps join together to make coral reefs. Coral reefs are important habitats for lots of sea creatures.

While lots of sunlight is important for coral reefs, too much sunlight can actually damage them. However, some corals make a chemical that makes them glow and protects them from strong sunlight.

Octopus

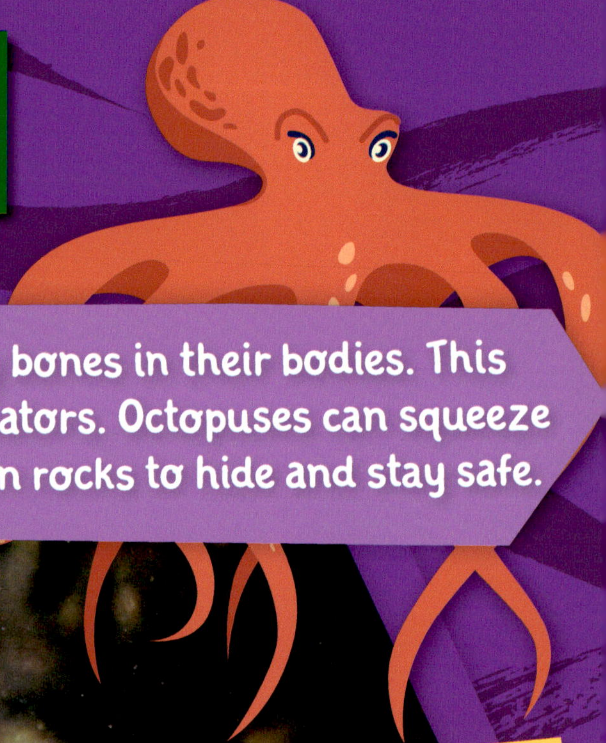

Octopuses do not have any bones in their bodies. This helps them hide from predators. Octopuses can squeeze into the small gaps between rocks to hide and stay safe.

Most octopuses live along the ocean floor.

Octopuses can also blend into their rocky surroundings. They can change the color and texture of their skin to match what is around them. This lets them hide from both predators and prey.

Anglerfish

Instead of going and looking for food, anglerfish get their prey to come to them with their <u>lure</u>. It glows in the dark and <u>attracts</u> their prey.

Anglerfish live in deep waters where it is very dark.

It can be hard to find food deep underwater. To make sure their prey cannot escape, anglerfish have teeth that curl towards the back of their mouth. Anglerfish teeth stop prey from swimming away!

Jellyfish

Jellyfish come in lots of different shapes and sizes. Some jellyfish are <u>transparent</u> so that predators cannot see them in the water. Others can glow brightly to scare off predators.

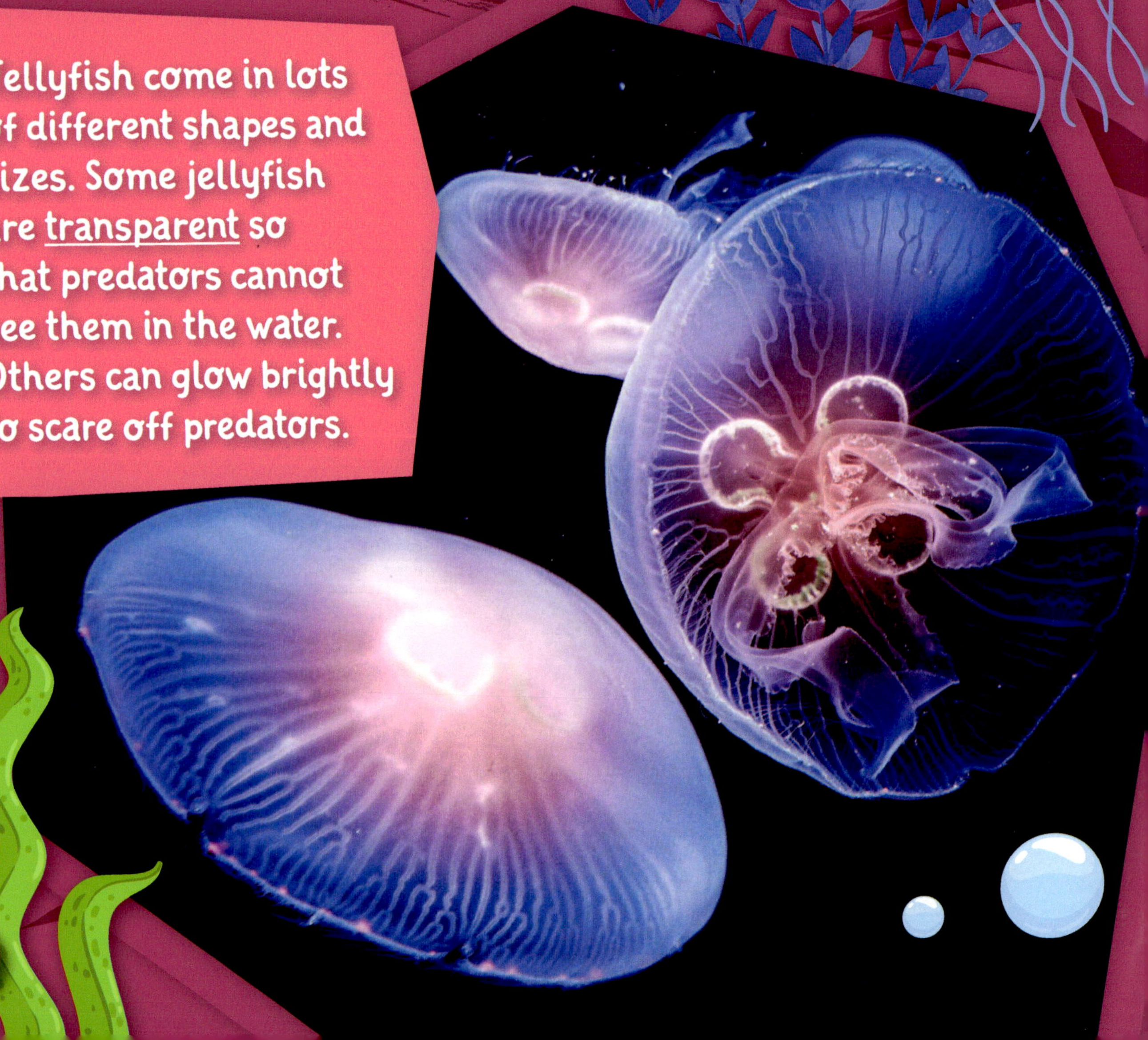

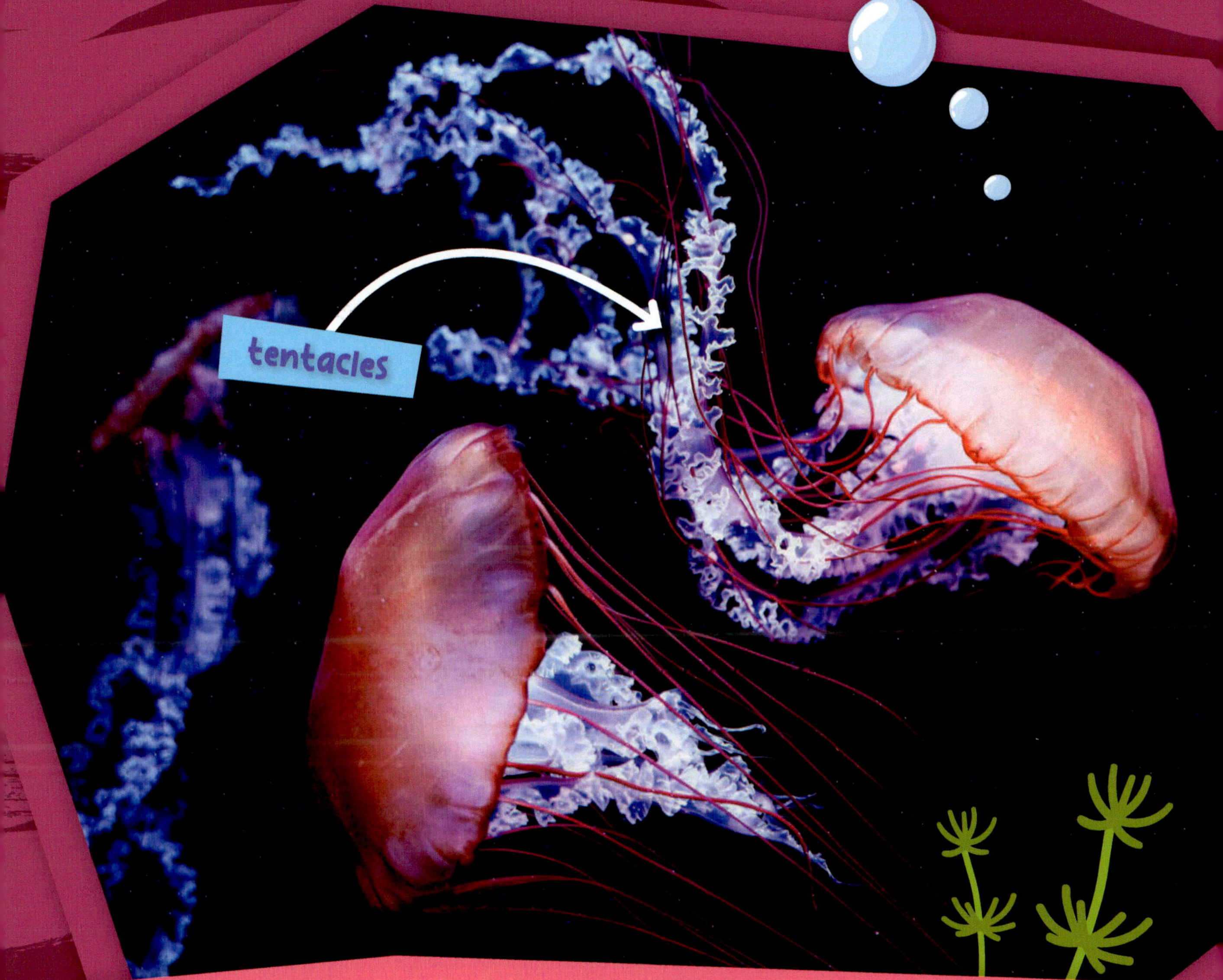

Some jellyfish have long tentacles that can give a powerful sting. These stinging tentacles can help jellyfish protect themselves from predators as well as catch their prey.

Animal Habitats

a desert habitat

Animals need to adapt to their habitats so that they can survive. This means adapting to their surroundings as well as the other animals that live alongside them.

Every habitat is different, and they are all home to lots of different animals. It is important that every habitat is protected and kept healthy. A healthy habitat means lots of healthy animals.

a mountain habitat

Glossary

adapt	to change over time to suit the environment
attract	to draw something in
chemical	matter that mixes with other matter to cause changes
dissolve	to mix matter fully into a liquid
lobe	a rounded part of an animal's body
lure	a body part that draws in prey
predator	an animal that hunts other animals for food
prey	an animal that is hunted by other animals for food
texture	the look or feel of something
transparent	able to let light pass through, or see-through

Index